Creepy Little Bastards

Concept and Writing by
Sean Elliot Martin. A.K.A. "The Lord of Shadow"

Illustration and Character Development by
Elizabeth Pallack. A.K.A "Elizadeath"
elizadeath.com

Layout and Cover Design by
Nick Wagner. A.K.A. "Nick Hanabi"
thepixelorchard.com

Copyright 2012. All rights reserved.

Good little children are precious like gold.
They say "Please" and "Thank You" and do what they're told.
But some little children are out of their minds.
And they leave a trail of corpses behind.

A is for Adam, who can't stand surprises.

B is for Benny, who sees through disguises.

C is for Carly, whose mom was a nag.

D is for Dennis, annoyed by a hag.

E is for Elfie, who made a mistake.

F is for Fanny, in love with a snake.

G is for Gerold and his favorite swing.

H is for Harold, who read too much King.

I is for Ingrid, who doesn't like cheaters.

J is for Janice, who learned from the skeeters.

K is for **Kyle**, whose new hat was stolen.

L is for Lenny, whose brain is still swollen.

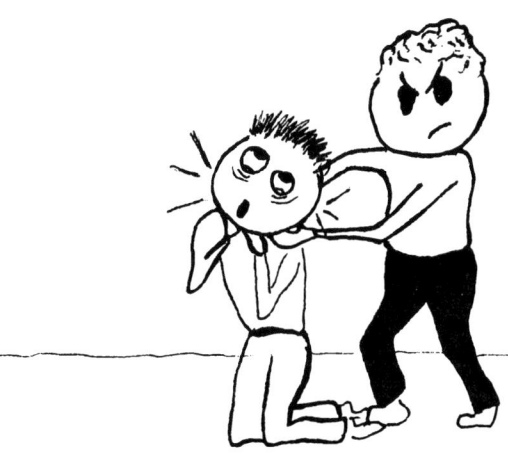

M is for Molly, whose dolly insisted.

N is for Nathan- the voices persisted.

O's for Ophelia- not her turn to drown.

P is for Paco, who really hates clowns.

Q is for Quincy, who needed a soul.

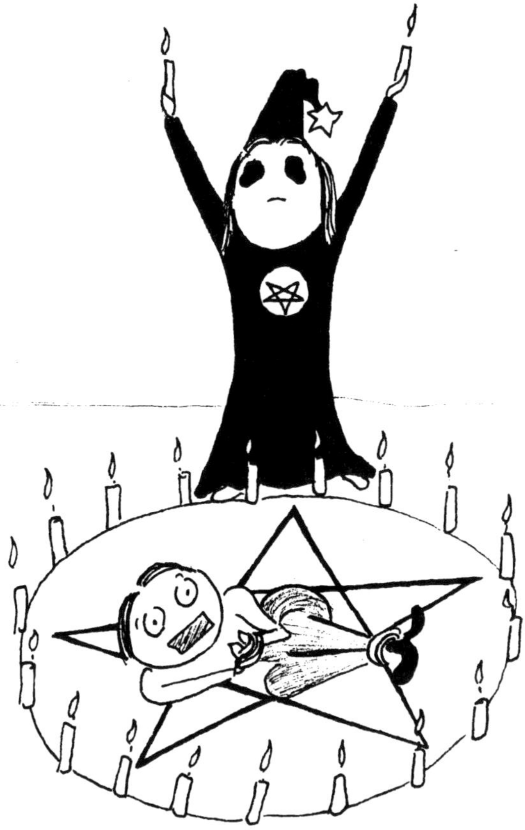

R is for Rita, who just loved to bowl.

S is for Salvador, painting in blood.

T is for Timmy, creating a flood.

U is for Ulysses' equestrian antics.

V is for Victor, made sick by romantics.

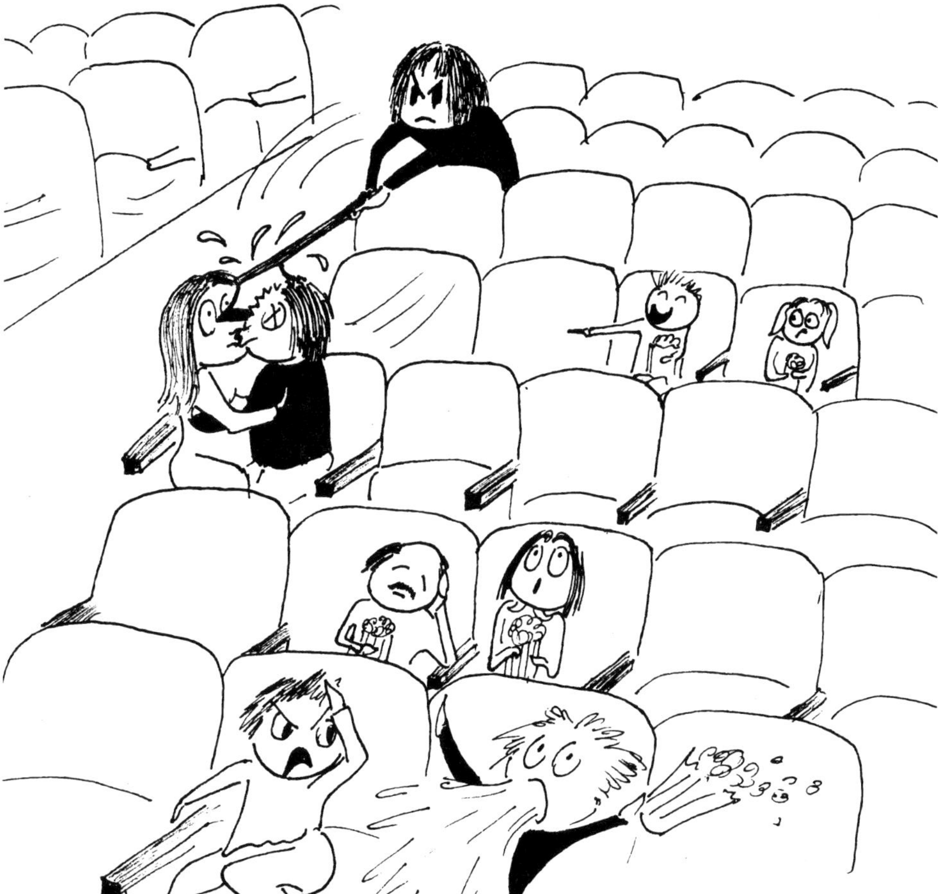

W is for Wallace, who wants to be knighted.

X is for Xenia, who wasn't invited.

Y's for the Yost Twins, sisters at play.

Z is for Zoe, who took in a stray.

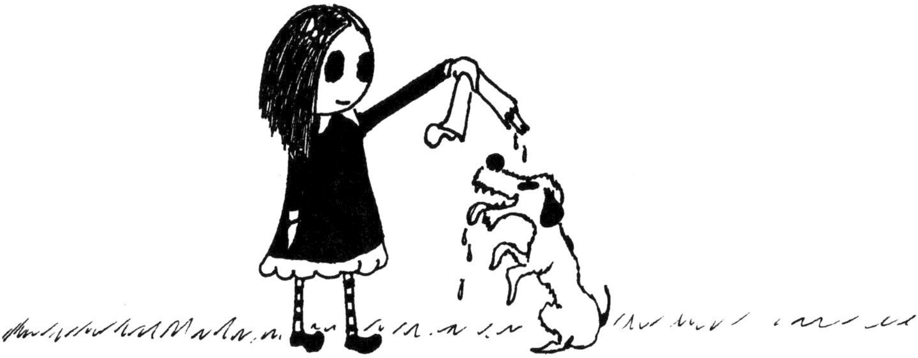

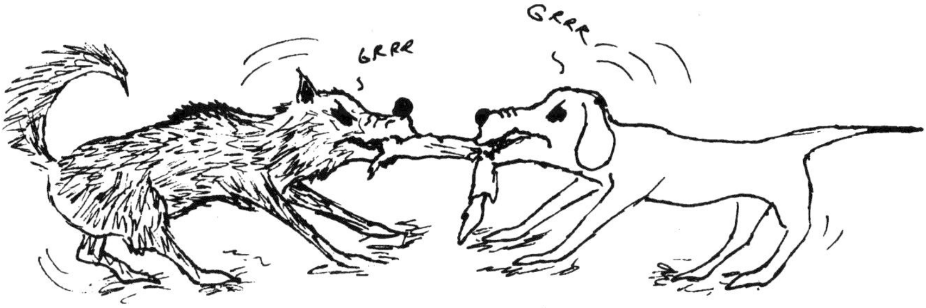
GRRR
GRRR

Most little children are gentle and sweet.
A joy to know and a pleasure to meet.
But always be wary of each little tike.
You never know which ones are waiting to strike.